YOU CHOOSE

CAN YOU SURVIVE the 1910 BIG BURN?

AN INTERACTIVE HISTORY ADVENTURE

by Ailynn Collin[s]

CAPSTONE PRESS
a capstone imprint

Published by Capstone Press, an imprint of Capstone.
1710 Roe Crest Drive
North Mankato, Minnesota 56003
capstonepub.com

Library of Congress Cataloging-in-Publication Data is available
on the Library of Congress web site.
ISBN 9781666390810 (library binding)
ISBN 9781666390803 (paperback)
ISBN 9781666390964 (ebook PDF)

Summary: The year is 1910. This summer in the Pacific Northwest has been the
driest anyone has seen in a long time. The weather is extremely hot and windy.
Crops are drying up everywhere. Then, in August, one of the biggest forest fires
in U.S. history is sparked. Will you join the fight to battle the fires and save
your town? Do you help lead others to safety or try to escape before the town is
consumed by flames? With dozens of possible choices, YOU have to decide how to
survive one of the biggest forest fires in history.

Editorial Credits
Editor: Aaron Sautter; Designer: Bobbie Nuytten; Media Researcher: Tracy
Cummins; Production Specialist: Whitney Schaefer

All internet sites appearing in back matter were available and accurate when this
book was sent to press.

Printed and bound in the USA. PO#5195

TABLE OF CONTENTS

ABOUT YOUR ADVENTURE

It's the middle of summer in 1910. You live in the Pacific Northwest, and rain has been scarce. July was extremely hot and windy. Crops and forest lands have been drying up. People are saying it's the worst drought they've ever seen.

Even worse, fires have sprung up all over. You hear they're headed your way. Are the firefighters prepared to take on the roaring fires? And if the fire hits your town, are you prepared to survive?

Chapter One sets the scene. Then you choose which path to read. Follow the directions at the bottom of the page as you read the stories. The choices you make will decide what happens next. After you finish one path, go back and read the others for new perspectives and more adventures.

Turn the page to begin your adventure.

Building small towns across the Pacific Northwest required a lot of wood from the surrounding forests.

CHAPTER 1
A WORLD ON FIRE

In the early 1900s, the United States was a growing nation. Towns were springing up across the northwestern United States. With them came railroads, new homes, and new businesses. All of this new building required wood. Forests across the Pacific Northwest were being cut down to meet the towns' growing demands.

In 1901, Theodore Roosevelt became president of the United States. He was passionate about nature and wanted to save the forests. Luckily, one of his advisers, Gifford Pinchot, loved the forests as much as Roosevelt. Together, they traveled the country, choosing the forests that would never be cut down. These lands became known as the National Forests. You can still visit them today.

Turn the page.

The U.S. Forest Service began at this same time. Pinchot was the Forest Service's first chief. The service recruited and trained forest rangers, who took care of the forests and acted as firefighters.

In 1910, there were fewer than 500 rangers across the nation. That summer, the Forest Service was put to the test in what became known as the Big Burn, the Big Blowup, or the Devil's Broom fire.

The Pacific Northwest region, including Idaho, Montana, Washington, and parts of British Columbia, has had an incredibly dry summer. Throughout July, small fires have been started by lightning strikes or sparks hurled from passing trains. Some fires were even started by firefighters on purpose. They used small, controlled burns to try to stop larger fires.

But then, on Saturday, August 20, 1910, a strong, hurricane-force wind blows over the mountains. The winds push many smaller fires together. They quickly grow into one of the largest and most destructive fires the region has ever seen. Nobody could have imagined a fire this size. How will you respond to the deadly blaze?

To fight the fires as a well-known forest ranger,
turn to page 11.

To help evacuate towns as a soldier,
turn to page 37.

To face the fires in Montana with your mother,
turn to page 71.

About 3,000 people lived in Wallace, Idaho, in 1910.

CHAPTER 2
SMELLS LIKE SMOKE

Your name is Ed Pulaski. You live in Wallace, Idaho, with your wife, Emma, and daughter, Elsie. You left your family in Ohio when you were 15 years old. Now you are 40 years old and an experienced firefighter, surveyor, blacksmith, and forester.

You started working for the U.S. Forest Service in 1908. Your boss is named Greeley. He's in charge of a large area covering Montana, Idaho, and parts of North Dakota.

As an experienced ranger, you know the forests and mountains around here better than anyone. You also know when the dry air smells like smoke, things are going to be bad.

Turn the page.

You're in charge of several rangers. Your unit has been successful at putting out some small fires around Wallace this summer.

On July 26, 1910, you wake up to a deafening storm. The thunder is loud, and the lightning streaks fiercely across the sky. But there's no rain. You have a bad feeling about this. In your experience, you know these electrical storms are likely to start forest fires.

To confirm your worst feelings, you receive a message from Greeley. It says that nearly 1,000 fires have started burning from Missoula, Montana, to Avery, Idaho.

Some of those fires are heading toward you. Are you going to fight the blaze? Or will you get your family to safety first?

To get your family out of town, go to page 13.
To stay and face the fire, turn to page 15.

While at the General Store, you smell smoke in the air. You look outside and see that the sky is gray. You have a bad feeling about what's coming. You know the fires must be spreading fast. An uncomfortable thought forms in your head.

"This fire is too big for us. We don't have enough men to fight it," you tell the shopkeeper.

The shopkeeper is surprised. "I've never seen you worry about a fire before, Ed," he says. "I think you could use a vacation."

"Maybe so," you smile. "Still, it's best to get out of town while we can."

As you head home, you tell a few more people they should leave town. But nobody is as worried as you are.

"We should catch the train to Missoula," you tell Emma and Elsie as soon as you get home. "Pack whatever you can carry."

Turn the page.

As you leave home, your neighbors chuckle. They think you're overreacting. But you don't care. Your gut is telling you that the worst is coming.

Later, you arrive in Missoula with your family safe beside you. That's all you care about. Then you remember reading a story in the newspaper. Several months ago Gifford Pinchot was fired by President Taft. As he left, he gave a stirring speech . . .

"We must win the war against fire," he said. "Not just to protect the forests, but also the forest service. Congress and the timber industry would love to close you down, but you're doing the good work of conservation. If we don't, those who come later will pay the price of misery, degradation, and failure."

You remember being inspired by Pinchot's speech. Now you feel guilty for leaving your post. You begin to doubt your choices.

To stay with your family, turn to page 18.
To return to Wallace, turn to page 19.

You know you can't leave your men to fight the fires without you. No one else knows the area as well as you.

You remember when Gifford Pinchot was fired. President Taft doesn't believe the Forest Service is necessary. Congress and the timber industry want to end the program. They want to keep cutting down trees to build towns and railroads. But you know that without the rangers, there would be no defense against the fires.

Turn the page.

Gifford Pinchot served as the head of the U.S. Forest Service from 1905 to 1910.

There's nothing you can do about politics and the government. But you can focus on the job in front of you. So you spend the next few days training your men. You show them how to chop down dead trees and clear the area around the town. You teach them how to light backfires that will hopefully stop the main fire from advancing.

You worry that you don't have enough men to fight a bigger fire. But your boss, Greeley, thinks your troop can handle what's coming.

A few days later, the air smells smokier than ever.

"A big fire is coming," you tell Emma.

"Are you worried, Ed?" she asks.

You sigh and nod. "Do you know that rock pile by the edge of the reservoir?"

"I do!" Elsie lights up. You took her there last summer to teach her to swim.

"If I'm away and the smoke gets thicker, I want you two to get to the rock pile," you tell them. "Sit in the water, and cover your heads with wet blankets. Wait for me there, and I'll come find you." You hope they'll take your instructions seriously.

"Can't you control the fire?" Elsie asks.

"We can manage the small fires," you say. "But I have a bad feeling that a much bigger fire is on its way."

Over the next few days, you notice the winds picking up speed. This worries you even more.

You must do something.

Turn to page 20.

As hard as it is to let your men fend for themselves, you can think only of your family's safety. Emma begs you to stay. And Elsie is too young to risk losing her father. So you stay in Missoula.

You decide to volunteer to get the fire reports out to the towns in the region. It's not much, but you do what you can to help.

A month later, you get some devastating news. Much of Wallace has been burned to the ground, and many of the men you worked with died fighting the blaze.

All you can do is live knowing that you left them to fight and die in the fires without you.

THE END

To follow another path, turn to page 9.
To learn more about the Big Burn, turn to page 101.

You kiss your family goodbye, knowing they'll be safe in Missoula. They know you must be with your men. They promise to pray for your safety.

You return to Wallace, and your men are relieved to see you. You spend the next few days training them to fight fires. You teach them how to chop down dead trees and clear the area around the town. You show them how to light backfires to help stop an incoming fire.

Still, you worry that you don't have enough men to fight a bigger fire. However, your boss thinks your troop can handle what's coming.

But in August, the air around Wallace grows thick with smoke. An uneasy feeling grows in your stomach. Over the next few days, you notice the winds pick up speed. This worries you even more.

Turn the page.

News from neighboring towns isn't good. A larger fire is gathering strength and could be heading straight for Wallace.

You send a message to Greeley. "Our town will not survive without help."

Your boss finally agrees with you. "Let's call for more men."

The Forest Service offers to pay any man 25 cents an hour to fight fires. Within days, a crowd of men arrive in town, including immigrants who don't speak English and prisoners who still have handcuffs on. But you don't care. You're grateful for their help.

You're in charge of about 200 men. They're kept busy by putting out small fires that seem to pop up every time you turn your back. You constantly travel back and forth to monitor your men, who are fighting several fires at once.

After a while, your men are exhausted. Many are inexperienced, and several of them are injured. Some quit, saying the job is too hard. Some prisoners even run away. Luckily, the mayor sends messages to the Army asking for help. Within days, soldiers arrive ready to go to work.

On August 10, 1910, the winds pick up speed. A soft breeze soon grows to winds blowing at 70 miles per hour. The wind blows down from the surrounding mountains and spreads the fires through the nearby towns.

Your first priority is to save Wallace. The town sits at the bottom of a valley, so the chances of it being destroyed are high. You begin to wonder if it's worth trying to save the town. Maybe it's better to just get the people out of there as quickly as possible.

To try to save the town, turn to page 22.
To get people to safety, turn to page 27.

You send your men to different spots around Wallace to stop the oncoming flames. Using shovels, axes, and other tools, you all try to push back the fire, but it's an uphill battle.

Embers of fire rain down into the valley. In the distance you hear the roar of the growing fire and the howl of the winds. It sounds like a monster is about to devour the town.

BOOM!

It's the *Wallace Times* building. The newspaper business had buckets of oil and grease lying around in open containers. When the fire got too close, everything went up in flames.

"Head over there, and do what you can!" you order some men. But you know in your heart that the building is lost.

BOOM!

Another explosion. This time it's the brewery. Next to that, a brand-new furniture store surrenders to the fire, too. You watch as the buildings go up in huge balls of flame. The buildings that remain are swaying from the intense heat. By 10 p.m., a third of the town is in ashes.

"Leave the buildings!" you shout, calling your men back. "We should go fight the fires at the edge of the forest instead."

"No! Stay and save the town!" the mayor insists.

You disagree. You feel sorry for him and for the people whose homes and businesses are destroyed. But you know that if the forest fire isn't managed, Wallace has no hope of surviving.

To keep fighting the fires in town, turn to page 24.

To fight the fires in the forest, turn to page 30.

In the early 1900s, fire engines were horse-drawn wagons equipped with firefighting gear.

Wallace's small group of firefighters joins you and does what they can. You must keep the fires from spreading through Main Street. But the flames keep leaping from building to building.

The horses pulling the fire engine wagon scream in fear. Your men stand back from the extreme heat, hoses in hand. But the water is barely having an effect on the fire.

The wind blows strongly. Two firefighters hold on to telephone poles to steady themselves. One of your men runs in from the edge of town.

"The fire is heading for the Sisters of Providence hospital," he sobs. The skin on his hands is blackened and burned.

You gather a few men and head to the bridge that crosses the creek to the hospital. By the time you get there, the bridge is gone. It's burning, too. Your heart sinks. All you can do is pray that the nuns and their patients will be safe.

In the distance, a train whistle screams. Trees in the surrounding forest crack and boom as they hit the ground. This feels like your worst nightmare.

Gathering your wits, you order the men back to town. The heat is so intense, you feel your skin burning before you reach the edge of Main Street.

Turn the page.

Four-story brick buildings, once the pride of Wallace, now sway like melting toys in the heat. Some brave townspeople are helping to move women and children away from town. Others are hosing down small fires around buildings, to little effect.

"It's no use!" you order everyone. "Head to the trains!"

Because of the roar of the flames, no one hears you. Flames swallow building after building and jump into the street. It's too late. Within minutes, you, your men, and much of the town of Wallace are gone.

THE END

To follow another path, turn to page 9.
To learn more about the Big Burn, turn to page 101.

Embers of fire rain down into the valley. In the distance, you hear the roar of the growing fire and the howling winds. You have no time to lose. You must get people to safety.

The four-story brick buildings around the town square—the pride of Wallace—sway back and forth from the intense heat. You've never seen anything like this.

Smaller wooden buildings go up in flames first. Then the *Wallace Times* newspaper building explodes. Debris flies out from buildings onto Main Street. People run in every direction.

"We should evacuate the town," you say to the mayor. He agrees.

Townspeople dash past you, carrying whatever they can from their homes and businesses. You and the mayor direct people to the train station.

Turn the page.

You notice rail workers have filled a tank car with water from the river and are using it to hose down the area around the tracks.

You call your men to you. "Let's do everything we can to save the railroad tracks and the train," you say. "This is the only way to save the people."

The mayor gives orders to the soldiers who have come to help. He tells them to assist in getting the women and children out of town.

"Don't let any men leave," he orders. "We need them to help with fighting the fires."

The soldiers hurry from home to home, telling people to leave as fast as they can.

There's one train ready to leave. The fire is getting closer. Your men hurry to clear debris from the tracks.

"We've done what we can here," you say. "Let's head out to meet the forest fire."

Your men are tired and scared. You try to encourage them by reminding them that this is the right thing to do. Although some won't return home, they bravely choose to follow you into the forest.

The railroad was the quickest way to get people to safety when the fire reached Wallace, Idaho.

Turn the page.

You gather a group of 45 men and arm them with axes and shovels. You make your way to the creek. The water level is low. On the other side of the creek is a wall of flames and smoke.

"Wet your scarves, and cover your faces," you yell at the men. The roar of the fire is so loud, you're not sure they can hear you.

For a few hours, you all work to stop the fire from crossing the creek. Some are badly burned and have no choice but to head back to town.

"It's too much!" you finally declare. "We have to save ourselves!"

"What if we lie down in the creek and hope the fire blows over us?" one man asks.

"Maybe, but I know a mining tunnel nearby. We can hide inside," you suggest.

To lie down in the creek, go to page 31.
To take shelter in the tunnel, turn to page 33.

You decide that lying in the creek is the best option. You release the horses and hope they find a way to survive. Then you order all the men to throw their scarves and sacks into the creek.

"Soak them up good," you tell them. "Then lie down in the creek and cover yourselves. Don't move until the fire has burned its way past this area. Good luck!"

You find a spot downstream. You lie in the cool water. It barely covers your head. Using your hat and gunnysack, you cover your face.

Occasionally, you lift the hat up to get a good breath. Before long, the trickling of the water is drowned out by the roar of the fire.

CRACK! BOOM!

Turn the page.

The loud sound of a tree falling tells you the fire is here. You think you hear someone scream, but you can't be sure. You're tempted to check on your men, but you know the best thing to do is to stay still.

It feels as if you lay in the water for hours. The water gradually starts to feel warmer. Is that your imagination? Then, another loud crack fills your ears, followed by a terrible pain. The world seems to go black.

The townspeople find your troop days later. You and your men were all killed by the falling, burning trees. The town mourns your deaths and is grateful for your heroism.

THE END

To follow another path, turn to page 9.
To learn more about the Big Burn, turn to page 101.

You lead your 45 men and two horses through the forest, skirting the worst of the flames. You know the mining tunnel is just a couple of miles from here. If you can get the men inside, you might have a chance to survive.

A terrible scream stops you in your tracks. One of your men fell behind. Sadly, he is killed by a falling tree.

"Keep going, men!" you cry. You must keep moving before losing any more men.

Finally, you reach the mouth of the tunnel. The entrance is wide and tall enough for the horses to enter. To your relief, the ground inside is damp. As you move farther in, you notice a small creek running along the floor.

"Soak your gunnysacks in water," you order the men. "Lie face down and cover your heads with them. Don't move until it's quiet."

Turn the page.

As they follow your instructions, you soak all available sacks and hang them up at the tunnel entrance. Using your hat, you scoop up water and put out the small fires burning the timbers supporting the tunnel. Your hands are scorched by the effort, but you don't stop. The lives of your men are in your hands.

The smoke burns your eyes, but you keep going. You ignore the pain. Eventually, you're unable to remain standing. You give in and lie down at the tunnel entrance, covering your head with your wet hat. Eventually you pass out.

Later, after the fire has passed, one man wakes up. He crawls out of the tunnel and runs back to Wallace to get help.

You and your men are taken to a makeshift hospital. Almost a third of the town has been burned to the ground. A day later, you learn that five of your men died from the thick smoke.

Although you're badly burned, you're alive. When you've recovered enough to move around, you're taken to see Emma and Elsie. They're thrilled to see you again.

After this fire, you invent a new tool. It's part axe and part hoe. With this tool, firefighters will be better equipped to clear the forest floors in the future. The tool is eventually named after you. It's called the Pulaski.

THE END

To follow another path, turn to page 9.
To learn more about the Big Burn, turn to page 101.

Units of Buffalo soldiers helped build several national parks in the early 1900s.

CHAPTER 3
BUFFALO SOLDIER

You are a soldier with the 25th Infantry, Company G. Your regiment, and the 9th and 10th Cavalry Regiments, are better known as Buffalo Soldiers. You're a proud part of these Black soldiers who served after the Civil War. Some white people treat you poorly because of your skin color. But you're happy to help protect people, wagon trains, and railroad crews along the Western front.

You've spent the last year building trails and roads in the Sequoia National Park. The Buffalo Soldiers are an important part of creating these parks across the nation.

You and 52 fellow soldiers have been sent to the small town of Avery, Idaho. Your company is commanded by a white officer, Second Lieutenant Edson Lewis.

Turn the page.

Forest fires in the area have been blazing for almost a whole day. Nearby towns like Wallace, Grand Forks, and Taft are also in danger of being destroyed. Your job is to help evacuate Avery as quickly as possible.

"Go house to house," Lieutenant Lewis commands. "Get people to the train station. Only women and children get on board. Keep the men behind. They need to stay and help fight the fires."

You walk to the houses just west of town. The sky is hazy, and the air smells of smoke.

By a hillside near the St. Joe River, you find houses tightly packed together. You go house to house to make sure the residents have left their homes. Most homes are empty. But when you knock at one door, a young woman answers. You also hear other voices inside.

"You have to evacuate," you say.

The woman stares at you. You repeat yourself. She shakes her head. Your first thought is that she doesn't want to leave home. A few other women gather behind her. They're all staring at you.

"Please, it's too dangerous to stay," you try again. "You have to leave."

The women speak to each other in a language you don't understand. Finally, one of them steps up to you and says, "You say we go?"

You realize that these women don't speak English. You'd heard that many immigrants were hired by the Forest Service to help with fighting fires. These might be their families. Using your best hand signals and short sentences, you explain that they all must leave.

Turn the page.

Finally, they understand. Several women and children exit the house. You point toward town and the train station, then continue to look for more residents.

At the very last house, you help a mother and her three children leave with some of their belongings. You lead them to the train station. Her eldest son, Tim, looks like a young man.

"All the men must stay to help save the town," you tell Tim. "That means you, too."

The mother begins to cry. "He's only 13," she says to you. "He's still a child, not a man. Please, spare him."

You're moved by their tears. You don't want to make him stay. But orders are orders.

To let the boy go with his mother, go to page 41.

To make him stay and help fight fires, turn to page 54.

"If he stays to face the fire, he'll surely die!" Tim's mother pleads. "Please, let him come with us."

Tears run down the boy's face. You feel bad for him. He reminds you of your own son, who's about the same age.

The train whistle blows. It's about to leave. You look around. Many women and children are rushing on to the train. Maybe if you shove this family into the crowd, no one will notice that the boy is almost a man.

"Hurry!" you whisper. "Try not to draw attention to yourselves."

You lead the family to the last car. People sit against the walls. In the middle of the floor are two men on stretchers. They're badly burned. They must be on the way to a hospital in the next town. Most women hang on to their children and try not to look at the poor injured men.

Turn the page.

Good, you think. *They'll be too busy avoiding eye contact to notice this boy.*

The family climbs aboard, and you wish them luck. The whistle sounds once more, and the train begins to move out.

As you watch the train disappear, you say a quick prayer for the family's safety.

"Did you find any men to help?" Lieutenant Lewis asks, walking up behind you. You're startled and try to hide the fact that you've just let a "man" leave.

"Not yet, sir," you say. "I'll keep looking."

"Never mind," he says. "Go and help clear the area around the houses on the hillside. We need to divert the path of the fire so the houses are safe."

Over the next several hours, you work until the air itself is pure smoke. You can barely take a breath. You feel exhausted.

"Men, it's too dangerous here!" the lieutenant calls out, just as you feel like you'll pass out. The roar of the fire is deafening, and he has to shout. "Move back to town!"

You see the flaming trees out in the distance. You can hardly believe how the fire gains on you as you run to town.

"We can't save the town," some men say. "There's one last train. Let's get out of here!"

The last train is just an engine with some flatbed cars. You climb on and find a spot to sit. More men arrive and squeeze on. Most of them are covered in soot. Some are slightly burned on their hands and faces. When all are loaded, the train begins to roll out.

"Wait! Wait!" A man comes running up, madly waving his arms. "The bridge is out! The tracks are on fire!"

Turn the page.

"What can we do?" the men cry. Some jump off immediately.

Others stay on board, willing to take the risk. "We'll get off as soon as we see the flames. Hopefully we'll find a way around it. We can't stay here. There's no chance of survival."

Your lieutenant gives your company the choice to stay or leave. "If you stay with me, we'll find a way to get through this. But take your chances if you want."

To stay with the lieutenant, go to page 45.
To stay on the train, turn to page 47.

As you watch the train pull away, you hope you've made the right decision to stay. You figure the lieutenant has more experience than you when it comes to fighting fires. You and a few men head back to Main Street in Avery.

"Our best bet is the St. Joe River," Lieutenant Lewis says. "We can shelter in the water until the fires pass by."

You all trudge down to the river. The air grows even hotter and thicker with smoke. Soon you can barely see your hand in front of you.

"It's jumping the river!" someone cries. You have no idea what that means.

Before you can ask, you can see flames ahead of you. Trees are being consumed by fire. The crackle and boom of the burning limbs sound like explosions. As trees fall, the ground beneath your feet rumbles.

Turn the page.

You and the other men don't even make it to the river. The fire is so great that it jumps across the water.

"Run for your lives!" Lieutenant Lewis orders.

You turn to run, but there's nowhere to go. The fire is spreading too fast. There's no way you can outrun it. Within seconds, you're surrounded by the blaze. You feel the searing pain as you're engulfed by the flames.

Days later, your burned body is discovered with those of the lieutenant and the men in your company. The townsfolk mourn your death and call you heroes for trying to save their town. Years later, a memorial is built to honor the bravery shown by you and your fellow Buffalo Soldiers.

THE END

To follow another path, turn to page 9.
To learn more about the Big Burn, turn to page 101.

You decide you want to get out of town and stay on the train. The first few miles seem promising. You even shut your eyes for a nap. But suddenly, the train's whistle blows.

"The track is blocked!" men cry, jumping off the flatbed, waving their axes. "We have to clear the debris."

You feel stiff as you jump off to help. Dead branches and even entire logs have fallen across the railroad tracks. The train can't possibly move any farther.

Progress is slow. You and the men clear a section of track, hop back on the train, and move down the path. It must stop every few miles. Each time, you hop off and clear the track of debris. At one stop, while working with two men to move a log off the tracks, there's a loud rumble from the hill above. You look up to see rocks and boulders rolling toward you.

Turn the page.

"Take cover!" someone yells. You jump off the track and run downhill. You hide behind a sturdy tree. But then you freeze when you hear a scream rip through the air.

"Jones is trapped!" someone yells.

A soldier you know well is trapped under a large rock. You jump in to help. By the time you move the rock aside, Jones has gone quiet. Your company has lost a good man.

Back on the train, you and the men are exhausted. Your throats are dry. Your hopes for survival seem slim. The little train stops barely a mile later. Another tree has fallen across the track.

Not again! you think.

You hop off and look around. In the distance, you glimpse the St. Joe River. Beyond it, the forest is a wall of fire, but that's not what you focus on. You long for the coolness of the water in the river.

"I'm done trying to clear the path," you announce. "I'm heading down to the river."

"Don't you see the fire beyond that?" a fellow soldier asks. "You'll be burned up for sure."

"Anything is better than what we're doing now," you say.

"It's only a little longer. We'll be in the next town soon."

You're not so sure about that. You know the next town is Grand Forks, and it's still some distance away.

"We should stick together," a fellow soldier reminds you. "That's how we all survive."

You're not sure about that either. What do you do?

To head to the river, turn to page 50.

To stay on the train to Grand Forks, turn to page 68.

"Can't you smell the air?"

You argue with the other men that it's too dangerous to stay on the train. "The fires have spread to the next town already. And if not, we'll be crushed by falling rocks or the very tracks will burn."

Your speech is convincing. The men decide to follow you down the hill toward the river. When you get there, you see that the water level is lower than expected. Just beyond the river, you can see the flames are coming closer. A forest ranger in your midst suggests that you all work to light a backfire.

"What's that?" you ask. "You want to light another fire? Isn't one enough?"

The ranger explains that if you set a line of fire before the main one reaches the water, the two fires would burn each other out.

This is new to you, but you trust the ranger. All the men work to set a long line of fire.

"Take cover in the river!" the lieutenant orders. "Cover your heads with your hats."

You and all the men wade into the river, find a shallow spot, and sit down. You soak your hats in water and watch the fires meet each other.

Turn the page.

As the fires raged near Avery, Idaho, some people stayed safe in the St. Joe River.

The roar of the fire is like thunder. You've never seen anything like this. But you can't watch for long. The heat is overwhelming, so you lie down in the water and hold your breath. The water is warmer than you expected. You fear the fire's heat could even burn up the river. Is that possible?

When you rise to catch a breath, you make sure your hat is covering your head. Slowly, with each new breath, the roar of the fires grows weaker.

"It's a miracle!" you hear someone shout, as you rise to take another breath.

You lift your hat off your face and notice there's nothing but smoke rising from the forest floor. The backfire worked. The fires burned each other out. Getting to your feet, you look around. All the men have survived. You can't believe your luck.

You all decide to follow the river east to the next town. When you arrive, you can't believe the stares you get. After everything you've done to try to save their towns, they still think badly of you and the other Buffalo Soldiers? It irritates you, but you're too tired to be bothered.

Luckily, the hospital staff doesn't care what color you are. You and the other soldiers are taken to the hospital. You spend the next few days recovering. You have burns to your hands, face, and the back of your head. But you heal quickly.

When you leave the hospital, the Big Burn is over. You're sad to hear of the number of people who have died. You're amazed that you survived such a great fire and glad you had a chance to serve.

THE END

To follow another path, turn to page 9.
To learn more about the Big Burn, turn to page 101.

"Please, sir," the woman cries. "If my boy stays here, he'll surely die! I beg you, please let him come with us."

Tears run down Tim's face. He reminds you of your own son, who's about the same age. You wonder how much trouble you'd be in if you disobeyed orders.

But before you can do anything, Lieutenant Lewis walks up behind you.

"I see you've found more help," he says, patting you on the back. "Good work, soldier."

Tim hugs his mother goodbye. She sobs in between telling him to stay safe.

"I promise to watch out for him," you say.

Tim is surprisingly calm. He tells his mother that he'll be fine and kisses his younger siblings goodbye. As the train pulls out of the station, he is very quiet.

"Stick with me," you say. "We'll both get out of here safely."

Tim nods glumly. You both go to join the other men. You're instructed to clear the dead branches around the town. It's backbreaking work, and the heat from the surrounding fires becomes almost unbearable. You keep Tim by your side and let him rest when he needs to.

Very soon, the air is almost too thick with smoke to breathe. You can just about see the flaming trees out in the distance. The fire is getting closer. You work faster. After another hour, Tim collapses from exhaustion. You help him to his feet and head back to town to see the medic.

"Men, it's too dangerous!" the lieutenant calls out as you near the makeshift hospital tent. The roar of the fire is deafening, and he has to shout. "There's one last train. Let's get out of here!"

Turn the page.

The last train has only flatbed cars. You climb on with Tim by your side and find a spot to sit. More men arrive and squeeze on too. They're covered in soot, with burns on their hands and faces. When all are loaded, the train rolls out.

The going is slow at first. You shut your eyes for a moment to rest. It feels as if you haven't slept in days. But then you're woken by shouts of dismay.

"The tracks ahead are on fire!" someone cries.

The train screeches to a halt and several men, including you, jump off the flatbed. You've barely left Avery, but about one hundred yards away, burnt trees have fallen across the tracks. The forest beyond crackles with a terrifying roar.

"What shall we do?" people cry. Many voices rise to answer.

"We have to turn back!"

"We'll die! Avery is already burning!"

"Let's try to clear the tracks. We have to get to the next town." Several men head toward the smoking tracks and begin to clear a path.

"The fire has probably spread far down the tracks," the lieutenant says. "I'm heading back to Avery." But he allows each of you to decide for yourselves. "If you make it to the next town, try to send help our way."

What is the best way to keep Tim safe? you wonder.

To stay with the lieutenant, turn to page 58.
To try to get to the next town, turn to page 68.

With Tim by your side, you watch the men begin to clear the tracks. You can't help wondering if you made the right decision. But you don't have much time to think about it.

BOOM! A building at the edge of town goes up in flames.

"Where should we go?" you ask the lieutenant.

Lieutenant Lewis rubs his dirty face with burned hands. He's in bad shape, just like you. You have an idea.

"This is an old mining town, right?" you ask.

The lieutenant's face lights up. "Yes. There must be old mine shafts in the area. We just have to find the tunnel entrances."

One of the men from Avery jumps up. "I know where there's one." He dashes off in the direction of the fire.

You swallow your fear and give Tim the bravest smile you can muster. "It'll be safer there," you tell him, hoping you're right.

Tim doesn't question you. He just follows along. You think of his mother and the promise you made to keep him safe.

The men skirt around the fire and enter the forest. The smoke is so thick you can barely see ten feet in front of you. You hold on to Tim so he doesn't get lost. In a few minutes, you enter a clearing. There in front of you is an opening that looks like an old cave. The man who led you here waves everyone in.

It's cooler in the tunnel. You all cram inside, and you get Tim in as far as possible. The coolness doesn't last. Within minutes, the tunnel fills up with smoke, and it gets really hot.

Turn the page.

"Lie on your faces and cover the back of your heads," someone suggests. You all obey.

Everyone is coughing violently. You try not to think about suffocating. But when Tim begins coughing hard, you really worry.

"I . . . I . . . can't . . . breathe . . ." Tim cries.

Tim can barely stand, let alone walk. You remember that there's a river nearby. If you get Tim there, he might have a better chance at surviving. You want to ask your lieutenant, but you can't see anyone clearly in the tunnel. Either you take Tim to the river or stick with the men in the tunnel.

To go to the river, go to page 61.
To stay in the tunnel, turn to page 65.

Tim has passed out. You'll have to carry him out of the tunnel.

You throw him over your shoulders, and your back screams in pain. You didn't even realize that your back was burned. You focus on Tim's safety and somehow find the strength to move forward.

On the way out, you trip over a few bodies, but no one reacts. You say a silent prayer, hoping the men aren't already dead.

You walk for a long time. The fire rages around you. The ground and the air are searing hot. But you find a path, taking one step at a time through the dense smoke. Just as you're about to give up, you finally see the water.

You put Tim down by the riverbank. The water level is low, but it's enough for you to wet your hat. You pour water into Tim's mouth. He wakes up choking, but grateful.

Turn the page.

"Let's find a place where the water is deeper," you suggest. "Once the fire passes by, we'll be safe."

Tim obeys without argument. He trusts you, and that makes you more determined to save him.

You wade into the river where the water is up to your waist. You tell Tim to sit in the water up to his nose. You cover his head with his wet hat. You do the same. The only thing to do now is wait.

The water warms up as the fire gets closer. It takes all your courage to stay in the water. When you rise to take a breath, the roar of the flames shakes you to your core. But you know you must be brave for the young man beside you.

It feels like forever, but the fire eventually passes by. The silence afterward is almost painful. Looking around, you see the forest is gone. What's left are burned-out trees and smoke rising in curls. You don't move for many minutes.

When you feel it's safe, you give Tim a nudge. You expect to see his head rise from the water, but instead, his body floats facedown in the river.

"Tim!" you cry, as you flip him over. He's out cold.

You drag him to the riverbank and shake him. He shudders and coughs up a lot of water.

"Thank goodness! You're safe now, Tim," you reassure him. You throw him over your shoulder again and carry him back to town.

*   *   *

It's a miracle! When you get back, you see the fire has somehow passed by Avery altogether. There are no people, but the town still stands. You find an empty building and lay Tim down on a bench to rest. You collapse onto the floor and sit nearby, trying to catch your breath.

Turn the page.

Eventually, your fellow soldiers emerge from the forest. Somehow, many of them survived the tunnel. They crawled out and made it back to town.

By the third day, the fire finally burns itself out. Slowly, the townspeople return. Your troop of soldiers is hailed as heroes for saving the town. When Tim's mother returns, she's grateful you kept her son alive. You and Tim's family remain friends your whole life.

This is the last fire you fight. After this close call, you go home to your family. You spend the rest of your days telling people about how you survived the Big Burn of 1910.

THE END

To follow another path, turn to page 9.
To learn more about the Big Burn, turn to page 101.

You get to your feet, but breathing is impossible like this.

"Get down!" you hear the lieutenant's hoarse voice. "Keep your face close to the ground as— *hack–hack!*"

His words are interrupted by violent coughing. You go back to Tim's side. The boy is having a hard time breathing too.

"It'll be over soon," you reassure him. "Just take small breaths."

You try to follow your own advice, but it's difficult. Every breath chokes you. Slowly, the sounds of coughing and labored breathing in the tunnel stop. Are the men unconscious, or have they suffocated?

Your lungs feel as if they're on fire. You don't know how much more you can take. You say a desperate prayer for help. Then you black out.

Turn the page.

When you wake up, the tunnel is dark, but the air seems more breathable. You hear voices, and someone's boot nudges you at the waist. You groan.

"I've got another one!" the gruff voice says.

You feel someone pick you up off the ground. It feels like you're floating on air. The next thing you know, you're lying in a wagon that's bumping along a road.

By the time you realize what's happening, you find yourself in a hospital bed in Avery.

The fire is over. Miraculously, it bypassed the town and left most buildings standing. The nurse tells you that you've suffered minor burns to your back and head. But more seriously, you've breathed in too much smoke. The doctor wants to keep you in the hospital to make sure you recover.

"Where's the boy?" you manage to croak. Your throat feels like sandpaper.

"The boy is the only other one to survive," the nurse says. "No one else got out. I'm so sorry."

It takes you days to fully understand her words. Your lieutenant and so many of your friends . . . all gone. But you're thankful that Tim is alive. You're determined to get well and return to your family.

Slowly, life returns to Avery. The Buffalo Soldiers are mourned as heroes for saving the town. When Tim's mother returns, she's grateful you kept her son alive. You remain friends with Tim and his family your whole life.

This will be your last fire. You decide it's time to retire. You return to your family and spend the rest of your life telling your tale of survival in the Big Burn of 1910.

THE END

To follow another path, turn to page 9.
To learn more about the Big Burn, turn to page 101.

The train chugs on for several miles. Hope rises in your chest. You imagine that Grand Forks is a big town and that it will be safe from the fires.

The train stops every few miles while you and the others clear debris from the tracks. You must be getting closer to the next town.

But the farther you travel, the hotter and smokier the air gets. You look up at the hillside that rises beside the railroad tracks. A loud crackling in the trees sends shivers up your spine. You watch the boulders and rocks very carefully for any sign of movement. You sit in such a way that you can jump off the train at a second's notice.

The smoke grows so thick that you begin to cough violently. It feels like your lungs are on fire. Your focus shifts to the other men. They're also coughing hard. Their bodies shake in the effort.

That's when you hear it. It starts as a trickle, but quickly turns into a thunderous rumble. Then the air is pierced by the loudest CRACK you've ever heard. You look up to see rocks and burned trees tumbling downhill straight for you!

You barely have time to realize what's happening when your train is hit. The last thing you feel is your body flying through the air before slamming into the ground. Sadly, you'll never get to return to your family.

THE END

To follow another path, turn to page 9.
To learn more about the Big Burn, turn to page 101.

Turn the page.

Taft, Montana, was founded by a railroad company in the early 1900s. After burning to the ground in the 1910 fires, the town was not rebuilt.

CHAPTER 4
LONG WALK TO SAFETY

You are an eleven-year-old girl named Alice. Your father once said that he wanted to be of use to humankind. So you and your parents moved to Taft, Montana. There, your father is the only doctor in the area. He treats patients in Taft and several small towns nearby.

Most of the men who live here work for the railroad company. Their job is to blast through the mountains to make a tunnel for the railroad. Other men work in the nearby mines.

The hardworking men come from all over the country and the world. The town of Taft is known for its saloons. Many of the men get drunk after work every day.

Turn the page.

This isn't a suitable town for women and children, but your father wants to keep the family together. You live in a nice log cabin on the outskirts of town, by the river.

In early August, the weather is extremely dry. The trees are brittle, and the ground crunches beneath your feet.

One day, news arrives from the U.S. Forest Service. They say that everyone in Taft should evacuate because the forest fires are spreading fast. Your father has been tending to injured rangers in nearby towns, so you know this is serious.

On the morning of August 20, your father leaves early.

"I won't be gone long," he says. "Stay here and wait for me."

By lunchtime, rangers arrive at your doorstep.

If forest rangers saw smoke, they would use maps and compasses to determine a fire's exact location.

"There's a large fire heading this way," they say. "You should leave. The last train out is your best hope."

Your mother doesn't want to leave without your father. But she wants to make sure you're safe. She looks to you to help her decide.

To leave your home and look for safety, turn to page 74.

To wait for your father to return, turn to page 77.

The idea of being trapped by a fire scares you. "Father would want us to be safe," you say. "We should go."

Mother agrees. You pack quickly, taking only what's necessary. When you head into town, you see rangers walking the streets.

"Last train to safety! Please leave town right away," the rangers call.

Many people in Taft don't seem to take the warning seriously. Some women in colorful dresses climb aboard with you and your mother. But most people just stand outside their buildings and watch. Some even laugh as if this is all a big joke.

Two men who are clearly drunk try to get on the train.

"Sorry, mister," a ranger tells them. "Men need to stay and help fight the fire."

The men curse and get off the train as you settle into a seat by a window.

"We're heading into Saltese," the train engineer announces. "Put the windows up. It's mighty smoky out there."

Your mother shuts the window. You press your face to the glass. At the edge of town, men are starting a fire in a straight line. You tug at your mother's skirt and point.

"It's called a backfire," she explains. "They'll start a small fire and hope that the big fire will meet it. The two fires will burn each other out."

You're not sure it makes sense, but you don't know anything about fighting fires. As the train leaves Taft, you say a prayer for your father.

When the train reaches Saltese, more people get on. This town is in danger from the fires too. Women and children crowd the train.

Turn the page.

Hours later, the train pulls in at Missoula, Montana. You and your mother find a small hotel to stay in. She sends a message to your father to tell him where you are.

A week later, you hear that Taft was burned to the ground. Your mother is devastated when she learns that your father was a victim of the terrible fire.

The two of you eventually move into a small house in Missoula and find a way to make a new life for yourselves.

THE END

To follow another path, turn to page 9.
To learn more about the Big Burn, turn to page 101.

Although news about the fire scares you, you don't want to leave without your father.

"Father asked us to wait here for him," you say. "If we leave, how will he find us?"

"I think it would be best if you get on the train and get out of town," one ranger says, shaking his head. "But if you're staying, then head to the creek behind your house if the smoke gets bad. Bring blankets, and sit in the water. Keep your heads and backs covered and wait for the fire to pass. Good luck to you both."

That night, you wake to the sound of your mother coughing badly. You do your best to comfort her, but it's too dark to do anything. You keep her comfortable until the sun rises. By then, she is weak and unable to get out of bed.

"I'll go into town to get medicine and supplies," you say.

Turn the page.

Walking to town used to take only half an hour. But this morning, the air is so thick with smoke that you must stop every few yards to catch your breath.

When you arrive, it's very quiet. Doors and windows are shut tight. You head toward the General Store.

"Hey! Little girl!" someone calls out. Two rangers run up to you. "You need to get on the last train. The fire is coming."

You explain that your mother needs you, but they don't listen. They grab your arms and lift you off your feet. They take you to the caboose of the small train and force you into a seat.

"Please don't leave my mother alone. She's sick!" you beg them.

They agree to go find her. They jump off the train and head down the path toward your home.

As the fires drew closer, the air was filled with thick smoke, making it difficult to breathe.

You wait and wait. Someone blows a whistle again, and the train begins to pull out.

"Mother!" you scream, but the train is so packed with people that no one seems to hear you.

Should you ride the train to safety? Or should you get off to save your mother?

To escape the train, turn to page 80.
To stay on the train, turn to page 86.

You get up and squeeze your way past the other passengers. No one stops you as you open the back door. They just stare at you blankly.

Thankfully, the train is just speeding up. It isn't going very fast yet. You climb down the two steps at the back of the train and hang on to the railing tightly.

One . . . two . . . three . . .

You hold your breath and jump. You land with a painful thud and roll a few feet away from the tracks. Lying there, with your face in the ground, you notice the ground is very warm. You wonder if the fires have anything to do with this.

Getting to your feet, you stay low in case the rangers spot you. Skirting the edge of town, you run home. When you get there, your mother is standing at the doorway, waiting for you.

"The fires are near," she says in between coughs.

Remembering the ranger's instructions, you grab two blankets and head to the creek behind your cabin. The going is slow and the air is dark with smoke. You can't tell if it's day or night.

On the way to the creek, you pass a small cave.

"Let's take shelter in there," your mother says.

The cave is dark, and you're afraid there might be an animal inside. Is it safer than doing what the ranger instructed?

To hide in the cave, turn to page 82.
To continue on to the creek, turn to page 83.

When you enter the cave, you're glad for the coolness inside. You and your mother move in as far as you can. You huddle inside the cave with the blankets covering your heads and bodies.

But in minutes, the fires find you. The cave fills up with smoke, and it gets hotter inside. Your mother begins to cough again. It becomes too hard to breathe. Your mother suggests lying flat on the cave floor. You try that, but soon, you can't catch even a shallow breath. You black out.

When you wake up, you're in bed in your cabin. Your father is taking care of you. He has tears in his eyes. Sadly, your mother didn't survive. She breathed in too much smoke in the cave. Your heart breaks at the loss of your mother. But at least the fires are over, and you and your father have each other.

THE END

To follow another path, turn to page 9.
To learn more about the Big Burn, turn to page 101.

You remind your mother what the ranger told you. She agrees that he would know best. It's slow going, but you finally get to the creek. You find a good spot to sit in the shallow water. Then you cover yourselves with the wet blanket, leaving room to breathe. At first, it's not so bad. Then you hear a loud roar. The fire has arrived!

BOOM! CRACK!

Turn the page.

Trees catch fire, go up in flames, and crash down around you. Your mother scoots closer to you. Soon you're both under one blanket, hanging on to each other tightly.

"Don't worry, Alice," your mother reassures you. "Pray for a good outcome."

You shut your eyes, but you can't shut out the terrifying sounds around you. The water warms up, and there are loud splashes and hisses as the burning trees hit the water.

The ordeal seems to go on forever. But finally, all is quiet. You and your mother emerge from the water to find destruction all around you. You shiver when you see how close the trees came to smashing both of you. You head home and find another miracle. Your cabin is still standing.

Later, you venture out to town. But Taft has been burned to the ground.

There's nothing left. Many of your neighbors' homes have been destroyed too.

Without supplies, you and your mother have to ration whatever is left at home. As you both discuss what to do, there's a knock at the door. You answer it and find a wonderful surprise.

"Father! You're safe!" You can't believe your eyes.

"Thank God, you're both safe," he exclaims. "And the house is untouched!"

He has a wagon and a horse outside and says it's time to go to a safer town. You pack your things and leave your small house in the woods.

"We'll come back someday," your mother says as you take a last look at the cabin before driving away.

THE END

To follow another path, turn to page 9.
To learn more about the Big Burn, turn to page 101.

You sit in a corner of the train caboose and cry. Your mother is all alone. She won't even know where you've gone. You watch as the last stragglers of the town hop on after you. Most of the men look like parts of their skin have burned off.

BOOM! CRACK!

You stare out the closed window. Flames seem to flow down the hill into town. Burning trees fall like used matchsticks. Buildings go up in smoke. In the middle of town, some rangers are setting a line of buildings on fire.

"Why are they starting more fires?" you ask.

A man with some bad burns explains. "It's called a backfire. It'll meet the one coming down the hill. They should burn each other out. Hopefully that will stop the fire from traveling to the next towns. We must sacrifice Taft to save the others." He rubs his head gently. "If it works."

Just as the train is about to pull out, you catch a terrible sight. A man runs out of the saloon. He's on fire. A few rangers throw blankets over him and pat out the fire. They carry him to the caboose and lay him right beside you. You almost gag from the smell of his burned flesh.

As you leave Taft, you sob and pray for your mother's safety.

Later, the train arrives in the next town, Saltese. You hear news that Taft is gone—the backfire didn't work.

The men on the train jump out and begin discussing how to save Saltese. They ask for all volunteers to help. They'll take women and children, too, if they're willing. Otherwise, the train is headed for Missoula.

To help protect Saltese, turn to page 88.
To stay on the train, turn to page 94.

You decide that helping is better than doing nothing. You don't want to get farther away from your mother either. You volunteer to help the rangers.

A man comes running into town. "It's no use!" he cries. "There's a wall of flames to the west. And it's heading our way fast. We should leave."

His words take a moment to sink in. But by the time they do, the train has left the station.

"Half of you—turn hoses on the buildings," orders the ranger in charge. "The rest of you, follow me. We'll set a backfire."

You have a bad feeling. In Taft, the back fire didn't work. What if the same thing happens here?

But there's nothing you can do about that now. So you follow orders and help set fire to a line of dried trees and twigs. It's so hot, you wish you had stayed on the train. You pray this backfire works.

It's amazing to watch the backfire leap over a dried-out creek and meet the wall of flames. The explosion of fire is thunderous. You've never heard anything like it. You all run for safety in town, as the roar of the fires fills your ears.

More quickly than you expected, the fires burn each other out.

"It worked!" you yell. "Saltese is saved."

The next few days go by fast. Everyone shares all that they have. You spend a few days with one family in town, helping with chores and cleaning up the area. You long for news about your mother. But when you ask the rangers, they tell you to be patient.

To walk back to your home, turn to page 90.
To wait for news in Saltese, turn to page 92.

The next morning, you wake up thinking your mother must be worried about you. You leave the family a thank-you note and sneak out of the house before the sun rises.

You follow the railroad tracks back to Taft. The long walk is harder than you thought it would be. You stop and rest often, but the thought of your mother waiting for you keeps you moving forward.

When you finally reach Taft, you gasp. The buildings are gone. In their place are mounds of ash. Scorched and blackened trees crisscross each other on the ground.

The scene is overwhelming. Since the town is gone, what hope is there for your tiny cabin? Surely, your mother is gone now. You collapse onto the warm ground. Hours later, you hear horse hooves.

"Mother! Father!" You can't believe your eyes. Your parents ride up to you.

"Father came home and brought this horse and wagon," your mother cries, hugging you tightly.

You tell them how you helped save Saltese from the fires.

"I've always liked Saltese," your father says. "It's not too far."

You head to Saltese with your family. You can't believe your good fortune. Everyone you love is safe and sound.

THE END

To follow another path, turn to page 9.
To learn more about the Big Burn, turn to page 101.

The family you're staying with overhears your conversation with the ranger. They understand how much you want to go home. But they convince you to wait for news.

Every day, you run to the newspaper building where they post the latest news. As the days go by, people straggle in from neighboring towns. They're all in shock and dirty, and many are badly burned.

"Have you heard anything from Taft?" you ask them. "Or of the doctor?"

But nobody can tell you anything. Your heart sinks. Will you ever see your parents again? You should've walked home.

The town has no doctor to help the injured. You've watched your father treat patients. So you decide to pass the time by helping nurse the sick and injured.

Helping people eases the ache of waiting for your family. By the end of the weekend, you hear the fire is over. Millions of acres of land have been burned. There is an air of relief in town. Even the injured seem to recover more quickly.

A few days later, a couple arrives in Saltese on horseback. You can't believe your eyes. It's your parents! As you tearfully hug them, you exchange stories. Everyone's adventures are as terrifying as they are miraculous. You and your parents have survived the worst fire in recent U.S. history.

THE END

To follow another path, turn to page 9.
To learn more about the Big Burn, turn to page 101.

You're about to jump off the train to help the firefighters, but a woman sitting next to you pulls you back.

"Best to stay on board and head to safety," she says harshly. "You'll only get in the men's way. Then they'll have to waste time saving you, too."

You're insulted by her words, but you don't have the courage to argue. So you stay aboard the train.

But within minutes of leaving Saltese, the train screeches to a halt. You climb out to see what's going on.

"The bridge ahead is out," someone calls out. "We have to head back."

Others argue that it's possible to walk into the valley, under the bridge, and get to Missoula.

"That's over one hundred miles!" a woman shouts. "How would the children walk that far?"

You stay in your seat and try not to cry. The burned man on the floor in front of you dies from his injuries. Everything seems hopeless.

Some men and several women decide they're going to walk to Missoula. Others want to head back to Saltese and help save it. It's not far.

To walk to Missoula, turn to page 96.
To go back to Saltese, turn to page 98.

Many people suffered severe burns during the fires of 1910.

You go with the group of people who are heading to Missoula. Following the train tracks, you can see where the fire has damaged the railroad. The going is hard, but you don't say much. Everyone is tired, and there's a sense of hopelessness in the smoky air.

Hours later, you come to the edge of a cliff. This is where the bridge would've been, but there's nothing there. Splinters of wood jut out of the blackened land. Ahead of you is nothing more than a giant gorge. As you stand at the cliff's edge and look down, you see another wall of fire crawl along the valley floor.

"There's nowhere to go!" someone cries out. "We have to go back."

You turn back. At first, weariness and hopelessness slow your steps. Then, you hear a loud roar. The fire has climbed up the side of the valley and is headed your way!

"Run!" people scream.

Everyone makes a mad dash to get away from the fire. But the air fills with smoke so quickly that you soon can't see in front of you. The thunder of the flames chasing you overcomes all your senses.

Your eyes are blurry from the burning smoke. You trip over something and hit your head on a rock. Dizziness consumes you. You can't catch your breath. The hot smoke burns your lungs.

When searchers later find your group, they're horrified to see everyone has been burned to death. Your parents recognize you only by your shoes that survived the fire. They mourn your loss for many years to come.

THE END

To follow another path, turn to page 9.
To learn more about the Big Burn, turn to page 101.

You decide to go with a group of people back to Saltese. The path back is hot and smoky, but eventually you all make it there.

When you arrive, you see the town has been saved. The backfire worked, and the fire's path has gone past the town. There is a quiet sense of relief as people work to clean things up.

People open their homes and share whatever they have. You spend the next few days helping nurse the injured. As a doctor's daughter, you've learned a thing or two about medicine. Your skills are appreciated.

One day, a couple arrives in town in an old wagon.

"Mother! Father!" You run with your arms wide open. It's a miracle! They're alive.

Your father hugs you tightly. "I reached home to find Mother there without you."

Saltese was a small mining town in western Montana near the Idaho border.

"You had us so worried," your mother adds, crying with happiness.

You tell them your story between sobs of relief. All that matters now is that you're reunited with your family. You're all safe and sound.

THE END

To follow another path, turn to page 9.
To learn more about the Big Burn, turn to page 101.

The fires destroyed much of Wallace, Idaho, and the surrounding forests.

CHAPTER 5
LESSONS LEARNED

The Big Burn of 1910 destroyed more than 3 million acres (1.2 million hectares) of land in two days. The destruction spread into Idaho, Montana, and Washington.

The U.S. Forest Service had been formed only five years earlier. Until that summer, the rangers had fought only smaller fires and weren't considered to be an important service.

But after the Big Burn, fire management and prevention became a topic everyone talked about. The policies made after that terrible summer are still in place today. Even the firefighting tool that Ed Pulaski invented is still used by modern firefighters.

A campaign was later launched to help make people aware of the dangers of forest fires. The most famous face of that campaign is Smokey Bear. In fact, the pinched hat that Smokey wears is modeled after the hats of the Buffalo Soldiers.

The 1910 fire didn't just burn forests. Several small towns were destroyed, including Taft, Montana, and a third of Wallace, Idaho. At least 85 people died. The fires were so large that smoke could be seen all the way from the New England region. Soot was found as far away as Greenland.

Despite the tragedy of this fire, many people showed their courage and bravery. Ed Pulaski was honored as a hero for saving his men. A few years later, he wrote a story about his experience in the fire and won $500 in prize money.

The Buffalo Soldiers were also hailed as heroes in many newspapers. Everyone was thankful they did their job so well to save people and towns.

Today fighting forest fires isn't too different than in 1910. Teams of wildland firefighters clear away dead trees and branches and dig long ditches called fire lines. When a fire reaches a fire line, there's no fuel left, so it will burn itself out.

Smoke jumpers parachute from airplanes into hard-to-reach locations to fight fires. In large fires, planes and helicopters help by dropping large amounts of water or fire retardant. This pinkish powder helps prevent fires from spreading.

Scientists study how fires start and spread. Although fires often happen in nature, it's important that people don't make things worse. For example, Smokey Bear reminds us to be careful with campfires. Don't start campfires when the weather is too dry. And only use safe firepits. Being careless in a forest can lead to terrible consequences. Be sure to play your part in keeping our beautiful forests safe.

MILLIONS OF ACRES BURNED

Scale	
3	
2.75	
2.5	
2.25	
2	
1.75	
1.5	
1.25	
1	
.75	
.5	
.25	

#1 IDAHO/MONTANA — 3 MILLION ACRES
1910: THE BIG BURN

#2 MICHIGAN — 2.5 MILLION ACRES
1871: THE GREAT MICHIGAN FIRE

#3 SOUTH CAROLINA — 2.5 MILLION ACRES
1898

#4 CALIFORNIA — 1.557 MILLION ACRES
2008: THE 2008 CALIFORNIA WILDFIRES

#5 OREGON — 1.5 MILLION ACRES
1845: THE GREAT FIRE

#6 ALASKA — 1.3 MILLION ACRES
2004: THE TAYLOR COMPLEX FIRE

#7 MONTANA — 1.295 MILLION ACRES
2017: "THE 2017 MONTANA WILDFIRES"

THE BIGGEST FIRES IN U.S. HISTORY

This chart shows the biggest fires in U.S. history up to 2017. Several of these fires destroyed millions of acres of land. Every year, it seems as if more fires happen, and more damage is done.

#8 WISCONSIN 1.2 MILLION ACRES
1871: THE PESHTIGO FIRE

#9 MICHIGAN 1 MILLION ACRES
1881: THE THUMB FIRE

#10 CALIFORNIA 972,000 ACRES
2007: THE 2007 CALIFORNIA WILDFIRES

#11 WYOMING/MONTANA 793,880 ACRES
1988: THE YELLOWSTONE FIRES

#12 OREGON 719,694 ACRES
2012: THE LONG DRAW FIRES

#13 IDAHO/NEVADA 653,100 ACRES
2007: THE MURPHY COMPLEX FIRE

#14 CALIFORNIA/OREGON 650,000 ACRES
1987: THE SIEGE OF 1987

#15 GEORGIA 564,450 ACRES
2007: THE BUGABOO FIRE

In 2020, California experienced five of its worst fires ever. The August Complex Fire was the largest. It was sparked by lightning strikes in August that year. Eventually, 37 smaller fires joined together to burn more than 1 million acres (405,000 hectares). Because it was so big, it was given a new name—the gigafire. It burned for three months, and nearly 3,000 firefighters worked to put it out by November. The cost of all this damage is almost unimaginable.

The fire season of 2020 was the worst the state had ever seen. More than 9,000 fires burned more than 4 million acres (1.6 million hectares) of land. More than 10,000 buildings were destroyed.

In 2021, California again experienced another very dry season that led to the second largest wildfire in the state's history. The Dixie Fire burned almost 1 million acres (405,000 hectares) in the northern part of the state and destroyed hundreds of buildings and homes. Smoke lingered in the air for weeks, affecting people's health.

Many experts believe the reason for such terrible fires is poor forest management and higher temperatures resulting from climate change.

OTHER PATHS TO EXPLORE

>>> Think what it would be like to be a young man living in Avery at the time of the Big Burn. Your family is about to leave on the last train. Do you stay to help fight the fires, or do you try to escape with your family? What would you do?

>>> Imagine you are a reporter for the *Spokane Spokesman-Review*, a newspaper out of Spokane, Washington. After the fire is over, you're asked to report on the terrible fires that took out nearby towns in Idaho. What do you expect to see when you visit these towns? How would you write about the brave people who lost their homes?

>>> What would it be like to be a ranger that came upon the Big Burn after it was over? You have a good friend who fought this fire and you believe with all your heart that he's still alive somewhere in the forest. How would you look for him? Where do you think he would hide to stay safe? What happens when you find him?

BIBLIOGRAPHY

"The Big Burn." PBS: American Experience. https://www.pbs.org/wgbh/americanexperience/films/burn/

Egan, Timothy. *The Big Burn.* Boston: Houghton Mifflin Harcourt, 2009.

Furgang, Kathy. *Wildfires.* Washington, DC: National Geographic Kids, 2015.

"The Great Fire of 1910." U.S. Department of Agriculture: Forest Service. https://www.fs.usda.gov/Internet/FSE_DOCUMENTS/stelprdb5444731.pdf

Pulaski, E.C. "Surrounded by Forest Fires: My Most Exciting Experience as a Forest Ranger." Forest History Society. https://foresthistory.org/wp-content/uploads/2017/02/Surrounded-by-Forest-Firest-By-E.C.-Pulaski.pdf.

Simon, Seymour. *Wildfires.* New York: HarperCollins Children's Books, 2016.

"WFSTAR: The Fires of 1910." National Wildlife Coordinating Group, April 13, 2018. https://www.youtube.com/watch?v=Aa71l-t8bJw

"When the Mountains Roared: Stories of the 1910 Fire." U.S. Department of Agriculture: Forest Service. https://www.fs.usda.gov/FSE_DOCUMENTS/fsm9_018977.pdf

GLOSSARY

conservation (kahn-suhr-VAY-shuhn)—wise use of natural resources while protecting animals and the environment

degradation (deh-gruh-DAY-shuhn)—gradual decline and wearing down of something over time

evacuate (ih-VAH-kyuh-wayt)—to leave an area during a time of danger

fire retardant (FYR rih-TAR-duhnt)—a chemical spread over a forest by an airplane to keep a wildfire from spreading

immigrant (IH-muh-gruhnt)—a person who leaves one country and settles in another

recruit (rih-KROOT)—to convince someone to join the military or an organization

regiment (REH-juh-muhnt)—a large group of soldiers who fight together as a unit

reservoir (REH-zur-vwahr)—an artificial lake that holds large amounts of water

surveyor (suhr-VAY-uhr)—someone who measures the shape, area, and elevation of land using special instruments

timber industry (TIM-buhr IN-duh-stree)—the business of cutting down trees to harvest wood used for buildings and other structures

READ MORE

Braun, Eric. *Can You Save a Tropical Rain Forest?* North Mankato, MN: Capstone, 2021.

Potenza, Alessandra. *All About Wildfires.* New York: Children's Press, 2021.

Thiessen, Mark. *Extreme Wildfire: Smoke Jumpers, High-Tech Gear, Survival Tactics, and the Extraordinary Science of Fire.* Washington, D.C.: National Geographic, 2016.

INTERNET SITES

America's Worst Wildfire: The Big Burn of 1910
historynet.com/americas-worst-wildfire-the-big-burn-of-1910

Smokey for Kids
smokeybear.com/en/smokey-for-kids

Weather Wiz Kids: Wildfires
weatherwizkids.com/weather-wildfire.htm

ABOUT THE AUTHOR

Ailynn Collins has written many books for children, from stories about aliens and monsters, to books about science and nature, to books about the past and the future. These are her favorite subjects. She has an MFA from Hamline University and was a teacher for many years. She mentors kids who love to write stories of their own. She lives outside Seattle with her family and five dogs. When she's not writing, she enjoys participating in dog shows and dog sports.